To the Sky

A Hot Air Balloons

Coloring Book

Right-Handed Edition

By Lisa Marie Ford

Colored By

_____

_____

To The Sky: A Hot Air Balloons Coloring Book
Right-handed Edition
by Lisa Marie Ford
First Published Friday, June 16, 2017
ISBN-13: 978-1548132767
ISBN-10: 1548132764

Created by Pics By Lis
the Down on the Farm Studio

www.picsbylis.com

This book is available in two editions: Right-handed and Left-handed.
Other Coloring Books Available:
Many Meetings - A Nature's Curiosities Coloring Collection

For Adventure Explorers

Friendly Greetings!

Coloring has always been one of my favorite things to do.
I am a kid at heart and I color for fun; here, there, and whenever.

"Many Meetings - A Nature's Curiosities Coloring Collection" was my
first coloring book to be published and truly was a dream come true.

That collection, as well as this one, is available in two editions.
A Right-handed edition features coloring pages on odd pages,
or the right page when the book is opened.
A Left-handed Edition features the same coloring pages
on the left page when the book is opened to two pages.
These options allow the colorist to choose whichever edition
allows the coloring hand freedom to express best.

I endeavored to give every pencil, marker, or crayon a chance
to color in this book.

There are a variety of perspectives of hot air balloons, such as
sideviews, looking down on the tops of balloons, looking up at
the baskets and balloons as they take flight. There are also
many styles of balloons; featuring modern, historical, even fantasy.

As with all my creative works, I invite you to smile everyday; for this
wonderful world which God gifted us with is full of beauty,
creativity, amazing colors, and magical moments.

 Thank you kindly for coloring with me!
 Lisa

Time to break out the pencils and have some fun.

Turn on some toe-tapping tunes, relaxing instrumentals,
film scores, or classic songs. Listen to an audio book or radio show.
Share laughter and memories with a friend.
Or reflect with thoughts and enjoy the sound of silence.

Special Notes:

This coloring book probably works best with colored pencils or crayons.

We suggest placing card stock or cardboard under the page
when using wet media, like markers or paint.
Also, feel free to dismantle this book to color or paint
using your favorite easel or clipboard to hold the page,
or to frame your finished image.

When the imagination runs wild the
color choices and combinations are endless.
So have fun and color these pictures your way!

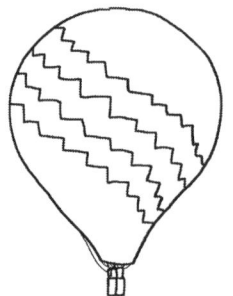

There is a page is for writing thoughts or for testing/blending colors.

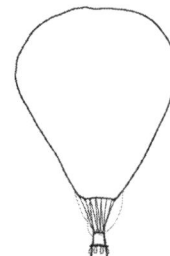

COLOR TESTING AND BLENDING
(OR DOODLES)

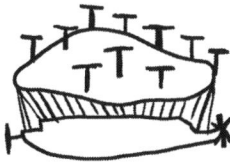

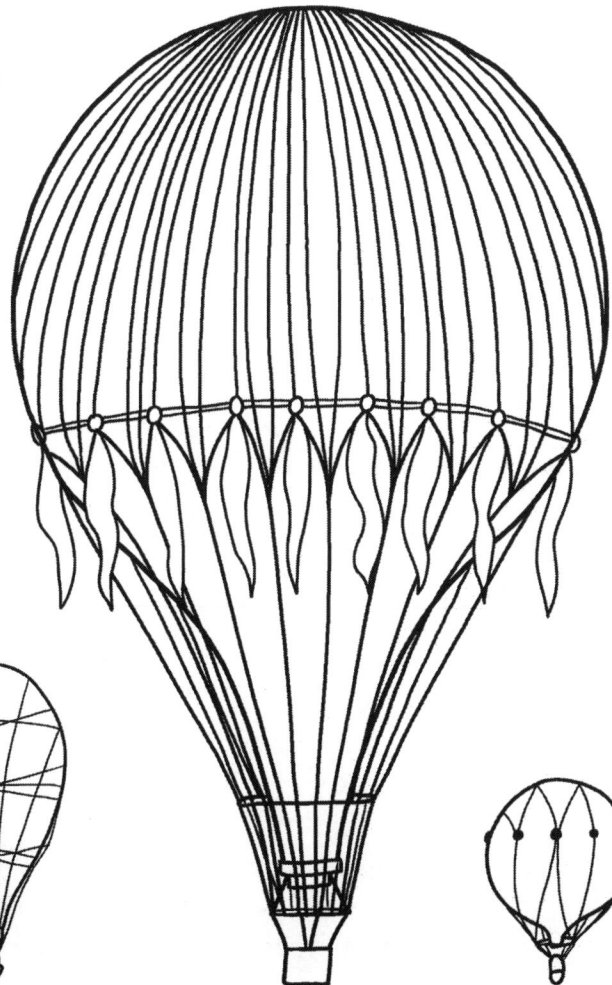

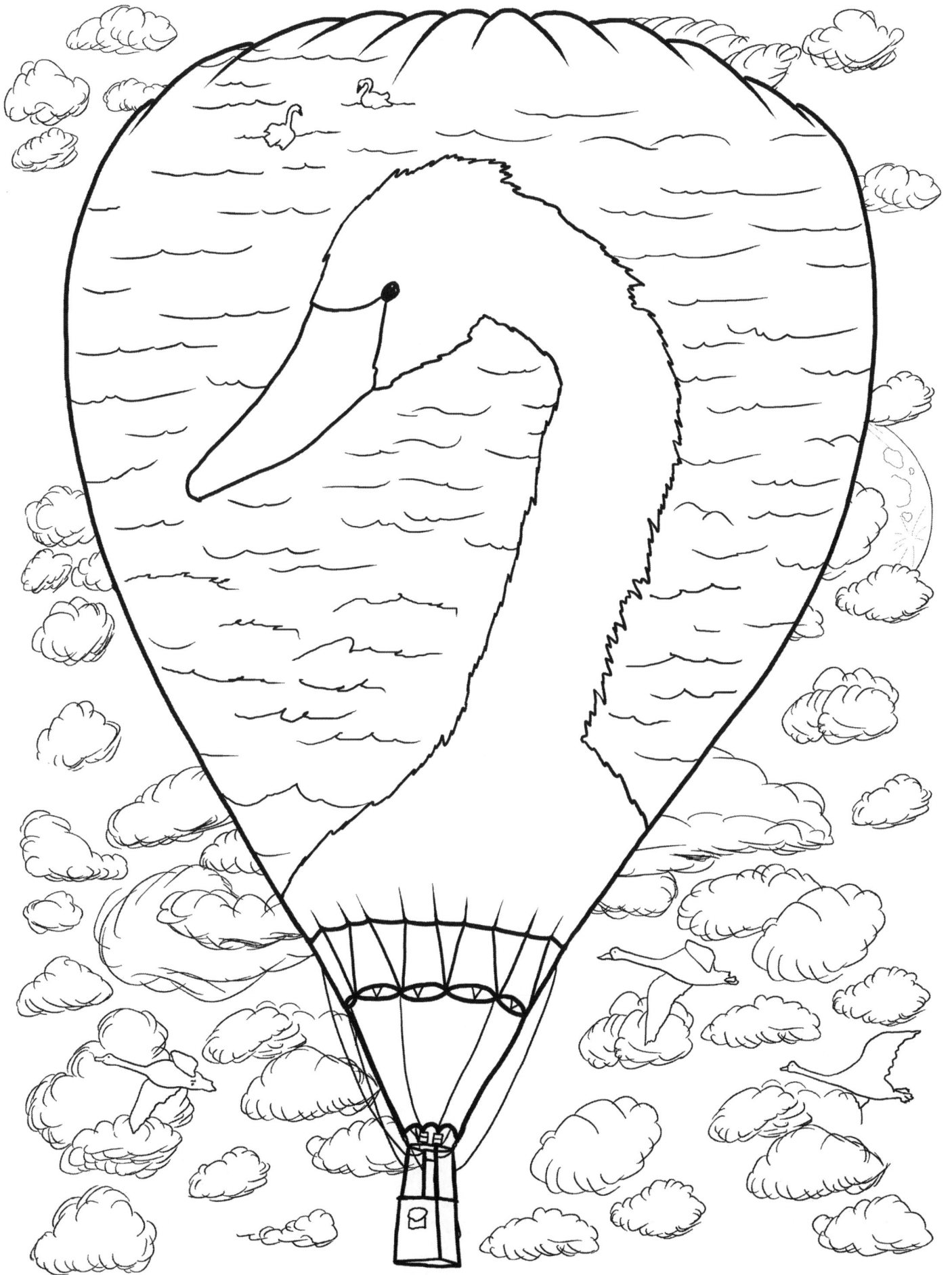

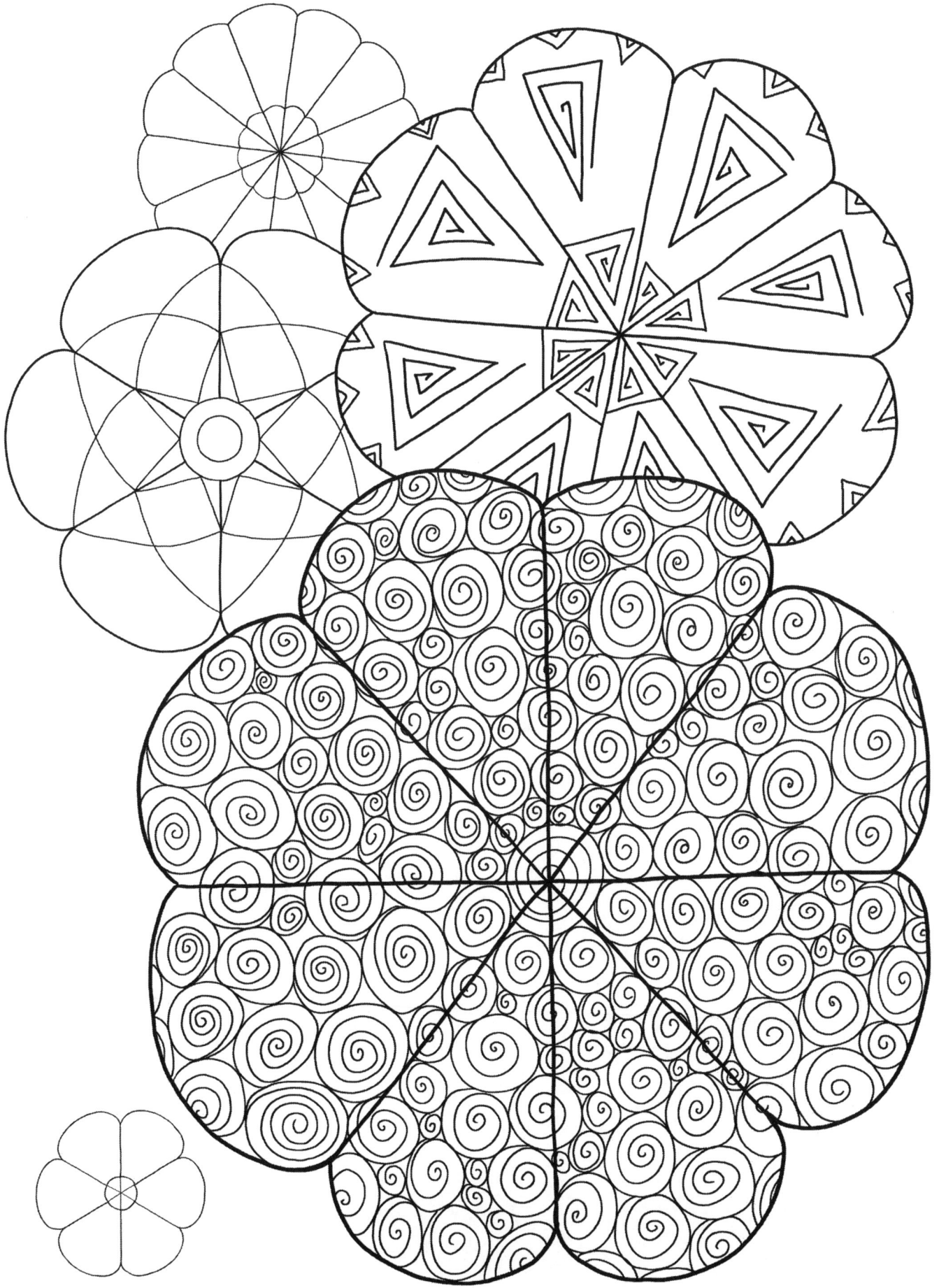

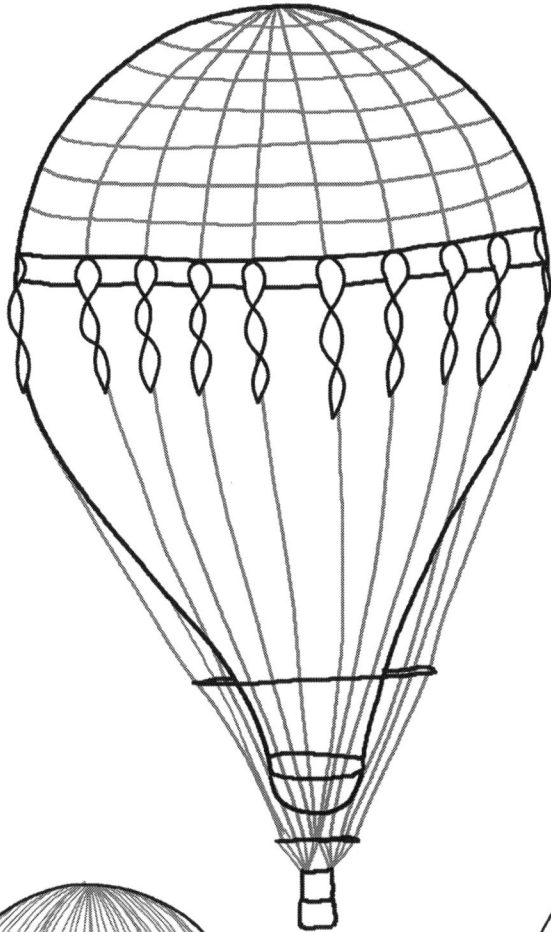

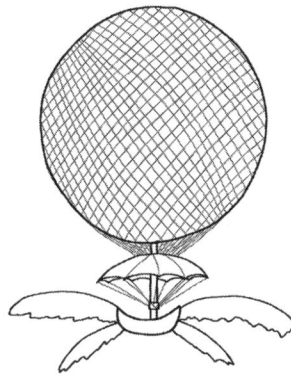

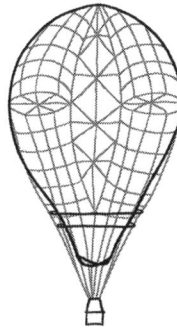

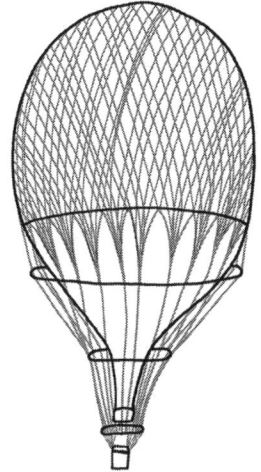

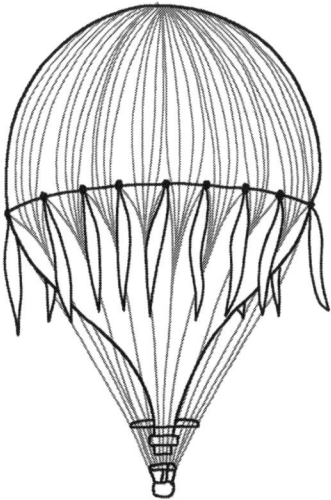

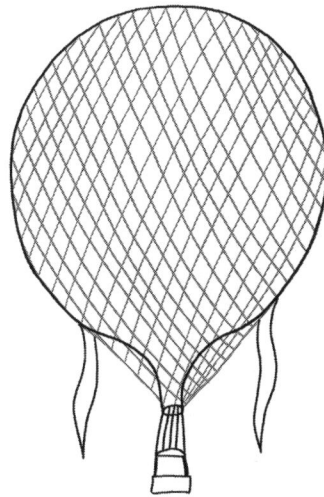

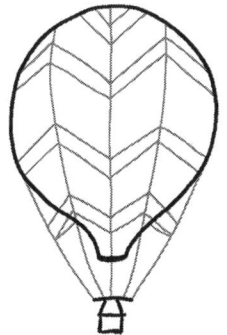

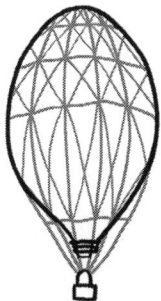

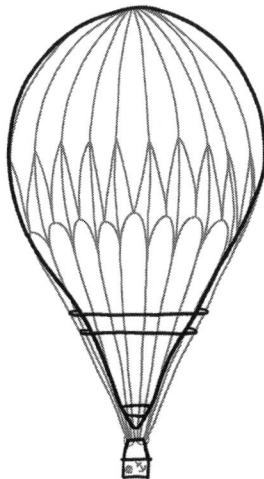

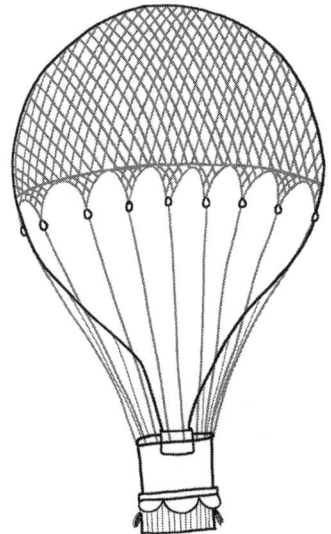

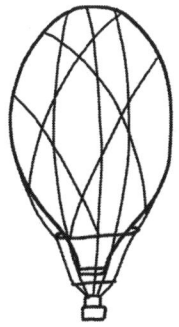

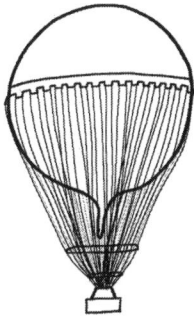

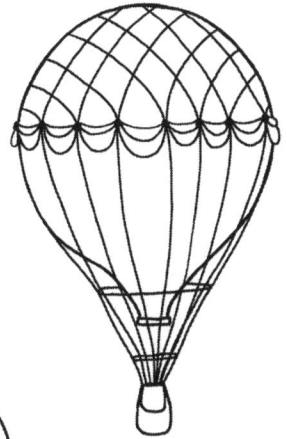

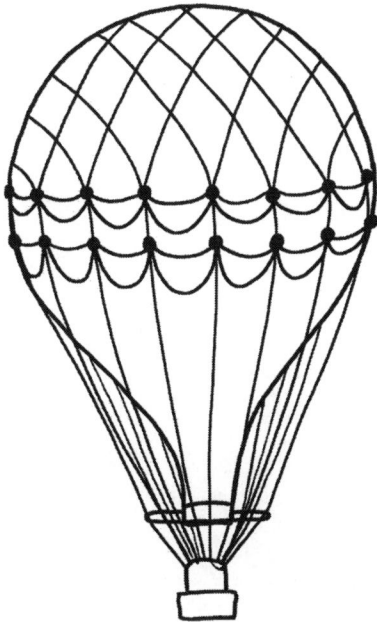

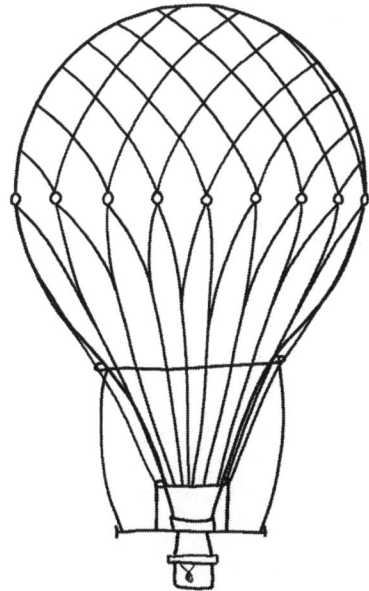

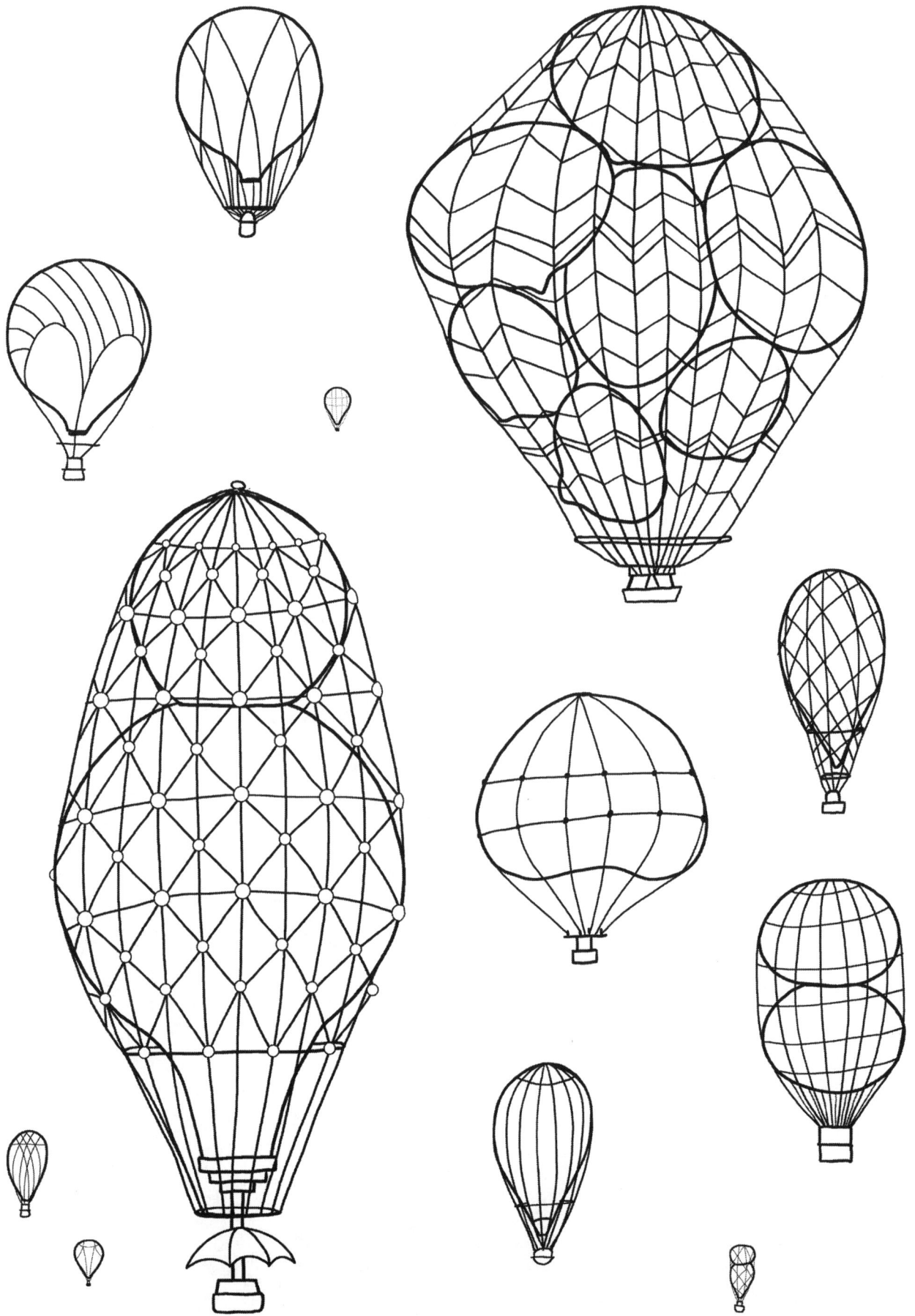

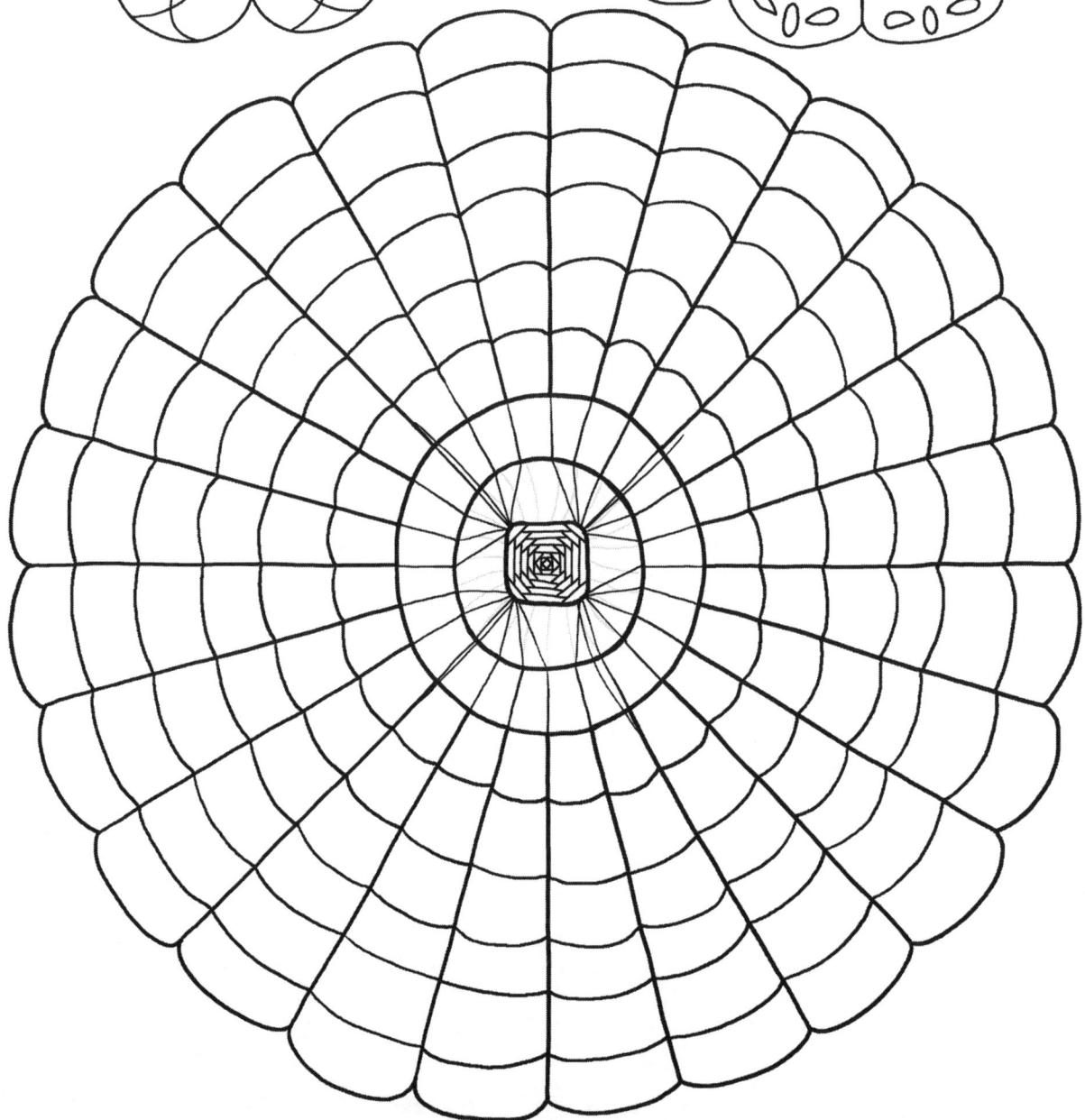

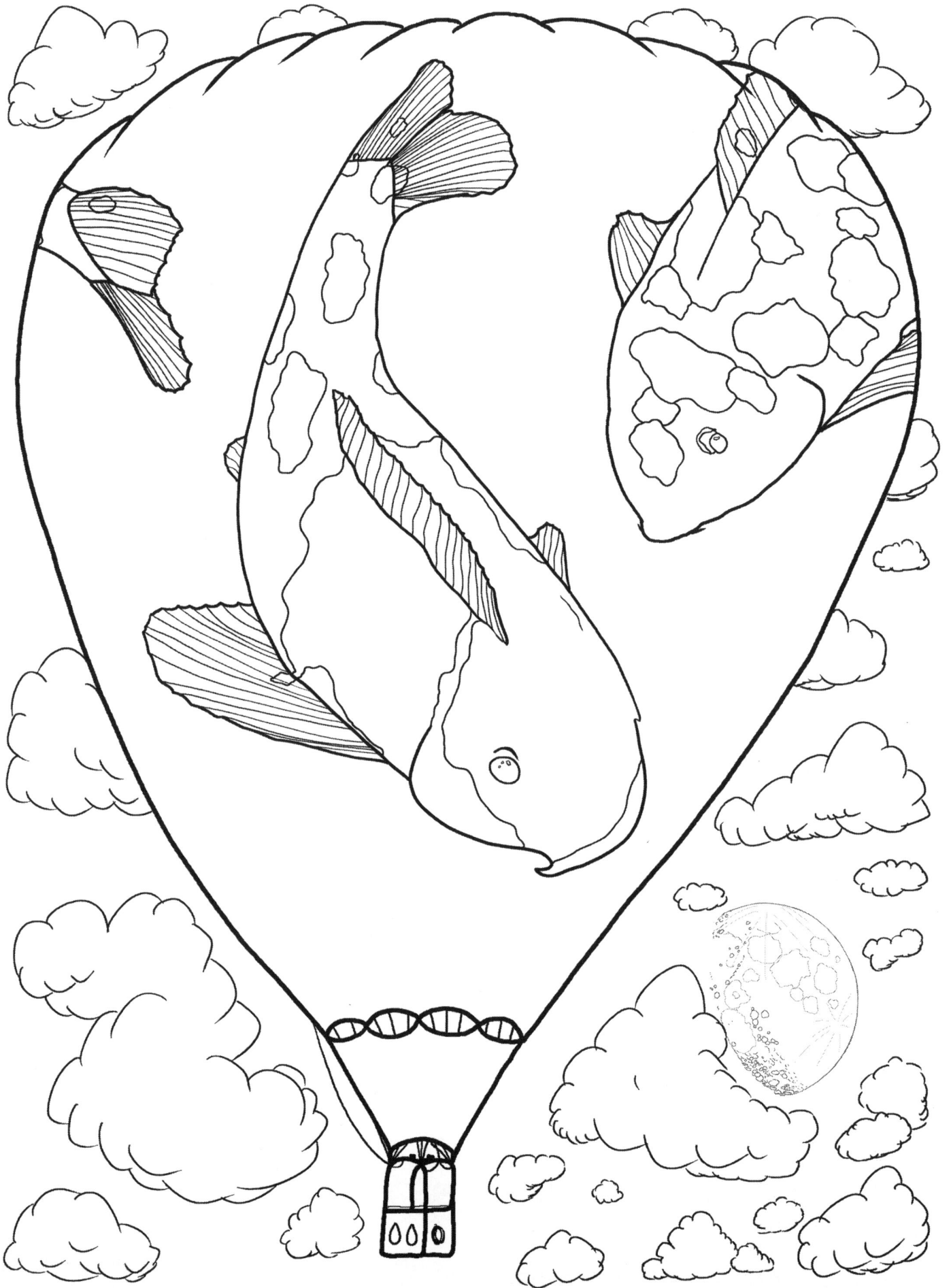

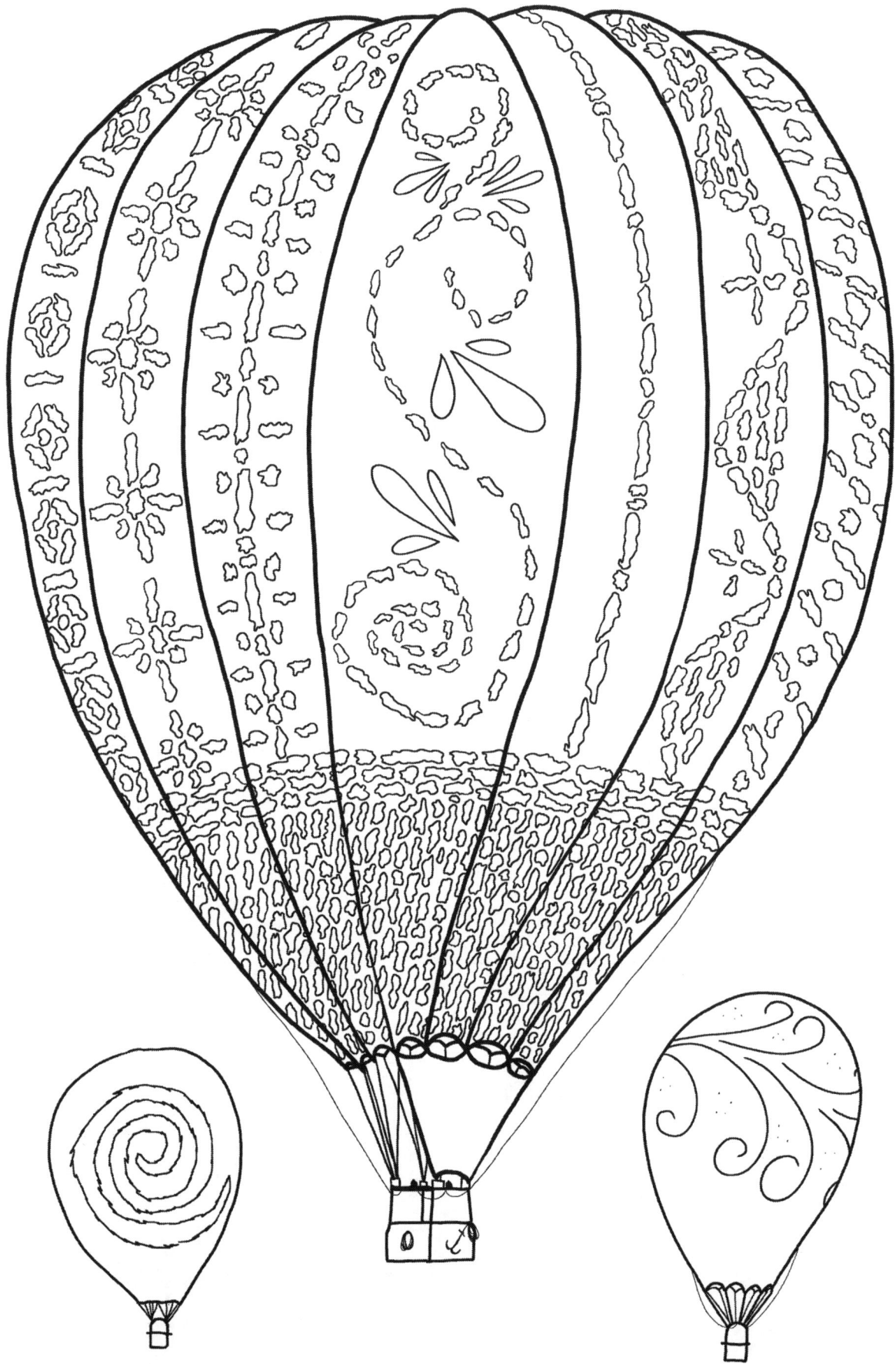

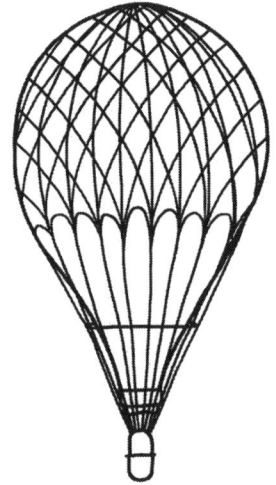

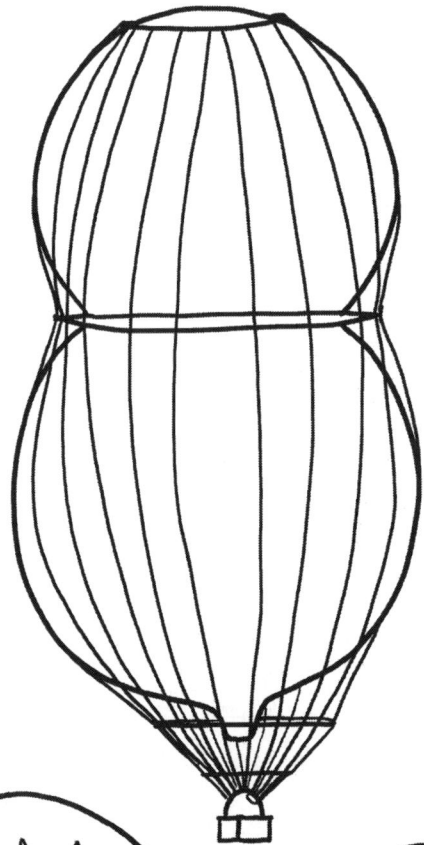

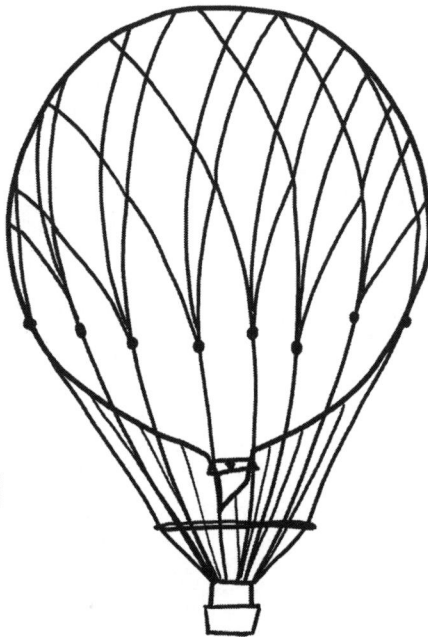

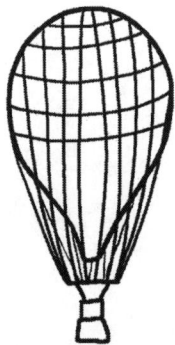

Made in the USA
Las Vegas, NV
12 January 2021

15833281R00044